D0549488

A MENAGERIE
OF ANIMALS

Illustrated Collective Nouns of Animals

Steve Palin

Taghan Press
Merseyside

A MENAGERIE OF ANIMALS

ISBN   1 871482 19 4

First Published 2000 by Thomas Lyster Ltd
for TAGHAN PRESS
28, Eaglehurst Road
Liverpool
L25 3QH

Printed in Great Britain for Taghan Press

A MENAGERIE
OF ANIMALS

Illustrated Collective Nouns of Animals

Introduction

Collective nouns were first recorded with any authority in *The Book of St Albans* of 1486, in which lists were entitled "*The Compaynys of Beestys and Fowlys*". The *Fowlys* were dealt with in the previously published companion volume *A Dissimulation of Birds*. This book deals with collective nouns of the *Beestys*! (or more precisely those relating to animals, fish, reptiles and insects.) The illustrations, in keeping with *A Dissimulation of Birds*, are of those creatures either essentially British, or at least feasibly seen within British boundaries and waters.

A collective noun is a word which describes a group or collection of things, variously called a *company term*, a *group term* or a *noun of assembly*. Not all apply to living creatures (for example a *clutch* of eggs), but those that do are some of the most interesting, both in terms of the word itself and also of its origins.

The origins of such collective nouns generally fall into four categories:

       true company terms
       terms which represent the young or progeny
       terms which represent characteristics
       terms which represent noises or cries.

Some, however, are entirely fanciful and yet others are the result of the mis-copying of scribes before the days of the printing press. There appears to be no logic as to why only certain collective nouns have passed into obscurity, although as a general rule, it is often the hunting fraternity which has kept alive those still in regular or even occasional use.

Many of these nouns which apply to living creatures were first recorded in the manuscripts of the Middle Ages, when social etiquette, particularly on the occasion of a hunt, demanded their correct usage. It is those creatures associated with the hunt (rather than those particularly inclined to be gregarious) which have the richest collectives nouns applied to them.

It must be emphasised in this volume, as it was in the last, that this book is not intended to be an academic work. Books such as C E Hare's *The Language of Sport* (1939) and James Lipton's *An Exaltation of Larks or The Venereal Game* 1970) have given the academic perspective on this subject. Rather, this work is intended to be fun. It seeks simply to provide a comprehensive list of the collective nouns of animals and to illustrate some of them.

The definition of **menagerie** in Chambers Dictionary is "a collection of wild animals in cages for exhibition". This collection is in pages.

ARMY OF FROGS

ARMY OF CATERPILLARS

Army of frogs and caterpillars

In his *Glossary* of 1828 Craven quotes *Bishop Hall's Contemplations*: "he that hath brought **armies** of frogs and caterpillars to Egypt can as well bring whole drifts of birds and beasts to the desart" (sic). This seems to be the first written reference to this collective noun and it has subsequently stuck, appearing in many later lists up to the present day.

Although caterpillars are often found together in large numbers, this is largely owing to them having hatched from the egg together and having shared the same food plants, rather than any particular tendency towards gregarious company. The collective noun is more relevant, perhaps, to their purposeful "marching " gait and the relentless laying waste of the vegetation on which they feed.

The application of the word to frogs is less convincing. Frogs can be gregarious and often group together in very large numbers, especially when mating, but the term **army** seems rather ill-matched. One theory is that it relates back to the plague of frogs in the bible which threatened a dynasty in the same way as might an army. An alternative collective noun for frogs is **colony**.

The common frog illustrated is the only species native to Britain. The caterpillars in the illustration are those of the puss-moth. When alarmed these beautiful creatures retract the head into their bodies and simultaneously display two large eye spots, wave a pair of red tentacles aggressively and shoot a jet of irritating fluid from a gland in their thorax. Just the sort of tactics you need from a member of the army!

Bale of turtles

Turtles might not immediately strike one as being British animals, and certainly they do not breed anywhere in Britain. A number of species, however, are seen around the British coast. These include the illustrated Green turtle.

Although female marine turtles spend most of their lives in the sea, they must return to land to lay their eggs. They do this by digging holes on favoured, selected beaches and depositing up to 100 soft-shelled eggs deep in the sand and then covering them over. Even if all the eggs were to hatch, the baby turtles must then run the gauntlet of predators before reaching the relative sanctuary of the sea (where only their increased mobility and greater number of hiding places protect them from a further battery of predators). However, because the beaches to which the turtles return are readily identifiable, egg collecting for human consumption is rife. This, coupled with the demands of tourism, has consigned many species to the endangered list. *Bales* of turtles are certainly not of the number they once were.

The origin of the collective noun is something of a mystery, but there has been some detective work! The collective noun for doves is *dule* (this comes from the French *deuil* meaning mourning and relates to the mournful sound of the birds coo-ing). It is thought that early scribes not only mistook *turtle*-dove for the turtle itself, but they also corrupted *dule* to *bale*. There is currently no better explanation!

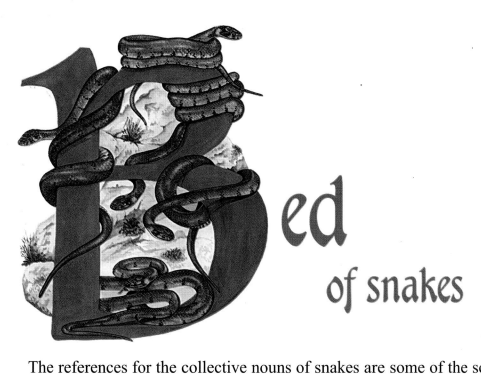

Bed of snakes

The references for the collective nouns of snakes are some of the scarcest. The author has found **bed** listed only in C E Hare's *The Language of Sport*, published in 1939. The other term, **den**, seems only to appear in the AA *Book of the British Countryside* list.

The words may serve to help reinforce many people's apparently innate but unjustified view of snakes - that of a cold, clammy serpent, poisonous and always ready to inflict harm on humans. The term **bed**, with its connotations of something to lie upon, may cause the un-informed to squirm. In fact snakes are warm-blooded and dry. They shun human presence and are often shy and retiring. Most snakes of the world are non-poisonous. Three species are native to Britain, only one being poisonous; the adder or viper. The other two are the now rare smooth snake and the illustrated grass snake.

Adders are rich in folk-lore, particularly as a creature of ill-omen (a reference to a different type of serpent in the Garden of Eden). To come across one and let it live was supposedly to invite bad luck. Consequently, snakes of whatever species have historically been killed on sight. An ash stick was supposed to kill an adder instantly, whilst their cast skins reputedly had medicinal qualities: to wear one inside a hat prevented headaches and tied around one's leg it was protection against rheumatism. A separate collective noun for the viper is **nest**.

The term **bed** has also been recorded as the collective noun for various shellfish, including clams, cockles, mussels and oysters. The latter has the term **hive** as an alternative.

CETE OF BADGERS

ete of badgers

One of the best-loved of Britain's native wild animals, "Brock" the badger still suffers from some persecution from badger-diggers. This, plus the claim that badgers carry bovine tuberculosis, together with an estimated death toll on Britain's roads of 50,000 animals per year prevent the badger from achieving the ubiquity that some may claim it deserves.

As well as the name "bawsen", the badger was at one time called a "gray" or "grey" referring to its hair colour. Thus in many lists the company term is referred to as "a *cete* of greys". The origin of the term *cete* is unclear. It is possible that it is the old Chaucerian word for city, and this is accepted as a more likely justification for the collective noun than the other theory that it derives from the Latin word coetus meaning a meeting or assembly. *Cete* appeared first in the *Book of St Albans* in 1486, although a *syght* of badgers had appeared in the earlier Egerton manuscript probably in error.

It is fairly widely known that the badgers' home is called a set or sett, but this should not be confused with the collective noun. Chambers Dictionary distinctly defines *cete* as the collective noun for badgers and *set* as a badger's burrow. One list also records an alternative collective noun for badgers as a *colony*.

Badgers are part of the family of animals known as mustelids. This family includes otters, martens, stoats and weasels. The badger has left indelible marks on the British countryside in place names such as Brockham, Brockenhurst, Brockholes and many more.

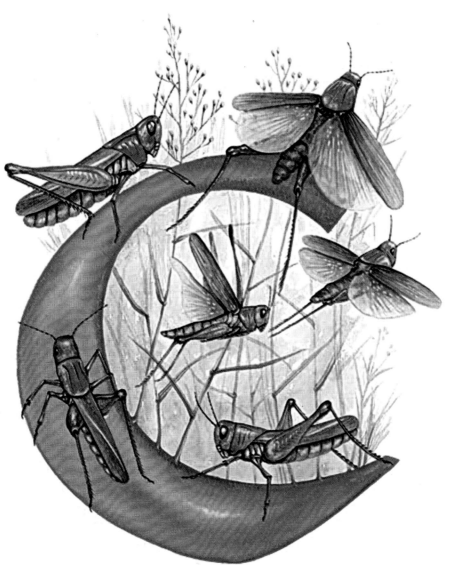

Cloud of grasshoppers

The term *cloud* applies to a number of insect species including the grasshopper. Those listed include flies, gnats and locusts. One of the dictionary definitions of the word *cloud* is "a great number of things" and certainly it seems apt for those insects listed above, especially when some appear in ethereal masses dancing in the air. The grasshopper is, in fact, the least likely to be seen in the air. It usually only flies when disturbed, but nevertheless can arise from the grassy places where it predominantly lives in fair numbers, or *clouds*. C E Hare in his *The Language of Sport* also refers to a Dutch source who quotes a *swarm* of grasshoppers.

The grasshoppers in the illustration are Common Green Grasshoppers, which as their name implies are common across the British Isles. There are eleven British species of grasshopper, only ten of which are able to fly. The flightless species is the Meadow Grasshopper and this is probably also the most common.

The "singing" of grasshoppers is a common feature of summer days in the countryside. It is produced not by any vocal chords but by the grasshoppers' legs, which have small projections on their inner side. These are rubbed up and down against each other, producing a chirping or scraping sound. The action is called stridulating.

DRAY OF SQUIRRELS

Dray
of squirrels

The word **drey** is fairly widely known as a term for the squirrel's nest. It has an alternative spelling of **dray**, but this word is also the more usual, and certainly the earlier, spelling of the collective noun for the young of squirrels. Confusingly, however, this term is also sometimes spelt **drey**.

The squirrel derives its name from its bushy tail which was once thought to serve as an umbrella; the Greek "skia" meaning shade and "oura" meaning tail.

Two members of the squirrel family are represented in Britain, the red and the grey. Only the red is indiginous, however, the illustrated grey first being recorded in Britain (of unknown origin) in 1828. The grey is native to North America and its first *recorded* release in Britain was near Macclesfield in Cheshire in 1876. Further introductions followed and their range increased dramatically. They have now displaced the red across most of England and Wales.

It was thought until quite recently that the greys' aggression towards the red was largely responsible for the demise of the latter. The latest opinion, however, is that the grey has a much more robust constitution than the red. Its digestive system allows it to avail itself of a more diverse range of food. The red is also more prone to certain types of virus. These two factors combined mean that following natural downward population fluctuations, the grey is better able to capitalise within a particular habitat location and over a period of time will become the dominant animal, ultimately excluding the red completely.

arth
of foxes

There are three collective nouns for foxes: *earth*, *skulk* and *leash*. The latter is a term applied to a group of just three foxes and is one of those collective nouns used for a wide range of animals and birds which are associated with the hunt in one form or another. The Egerton manuscript first listed the term *earth* as *nerthe* in 1452. The term is, of course, the name also applied to the fox's hole. The most commonly listed collective noun for foxes, *skulk*, was first recorded in *The Book of St Albans* in 1486 as *sculke*. The fox is not a gregarious animal and this term clearly relates to Reynard's stealthy prowling in search of its prey, traditionally around hen roosts!

In recent times the fox has extended its habitat to encompass towns and cities. The "urban fox" is now a recognised descendant of its country cousin, living as an opportunist both in terms of its daytime resting places as well as its feeding habits, which often include scavenging in dustbins.

The fact that so many folk-tales include references to the cunning fox is evidence of our intrinsic liking for this cavalier animal.

A very popular country belief concerning foxes at one time was one which stated that to rid itself of fleas the fox swam with a piece of lamb's wool in its mouth. To avoid drowning, the fleas would climb up the foxes body on to the wool, whereupon the fox would discard the wool together with the offending fleas. Scores of witnesses were reported to have verified this remarkable tale!

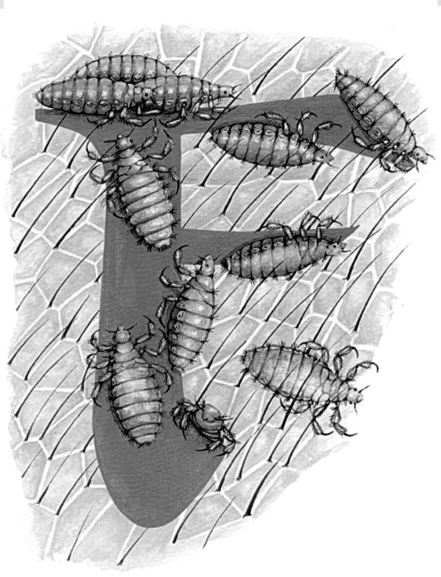

Flock
of lice

The Hors, Shepe, & the Ghoos is one of the earliest known books in England. It was printed by Caxton in 1476. The term ***flock*** as a collective noun for lice appeared in this volume, making it one of the earliest recorded nouns of assembly.

Flock is a term applied to a wide range of birds and animals including specifically camels, goats, sheep, lions (surprisingly) as well as beasts and birds generally. It is described by Hare as a "true" company term (as opposed to a term which represents aspects of the creature itself). ***Flock*** also has relevance, of course, to humankind, and is applied to crowds of people generally and more particularly to congregations of church members.

The true louse is a wingless parasitic insect. It is quite unrelated to the booklouse, the woodlouse, the freshwater louse and their relative, the sea-slater, none of which are parasitic. Rarely more than 3 or 4 millimetres long, the two main types of louse are the biting lice and the sucking lice. Biting lice are found mainly (but not exclusively) on birds, whilst sucking lice prey on mammals.

Human beings are not excluded from the list of sucking lice host species, and the head louse (illustrated) is still commonly found in children's hair. Stories of the "nit nurse" still abound! The other species found on humans is the crab-louse, preferring body (and particularly pubic) hair in which to make its home, from which it will bore into the skin with its mouth parts to suck the blood from its host.

Gam
of porpoises

Sometimes known as the common porpoise or puffing pig on account of its sneeze-like blow when it surfaces to breathe, the illustrated harbour porpoise is not as easily seen as some of its relations. It does not readily "bow-ride" in front of sea-going craft and shows little of itself at the surface. Observers who therefore get prolonged views of it are particularly fortunate and a fleeting glimpse is more usual.

Porpoises have four collective nouns associated with them (which they share with whales). Those better known include *school* and *pod*, whilst the term *herd* is in keeping with other semantic bovine connections such as cow, bull and calf for the female, male and young respectively. The word *gam*, as well as being another collective noun for porpoises and whales, has a definition as a social gathering of whalers at sea. Generally speaking, the term *pod* is used for smaller, perhaps family, groups whilst *school* or *herd* refers to the larger groups.

The collective noun *pod* is also applied to hippopotamus, seals, and whiting; *school* to fish and *herd* to many creatures, but those specifically listed include wrens, curlew, antelopes, asses, chamois, elephants, giraffe, goats, hares, seals and sperm whales.

Porpoises, like most cetaceans, have suffered in recent times from human interference. This has been both directly in terms of hunting and also indirectly from habitat pollution and degradation, as well as accidental capture in fishing nets. Nevertheless, the harbour porpoise is still the commonest and most widely distributed cetacean in British waters.

Grist
of bees

Bees have no less than eight collective nouns applied to them. Most people will be familiar with **hive**, which refers also to the place in which bees live, and **swarm** which is also a verb relating to the mass movement of bees flying to form a new colony. **Colony** itself is another term regularly used not only for bees but also for other creatures living together in a community. The collective noun **cluster**, which means a bunch, is aptly applied to bees specifically which are packed around a queen. The term **drift** is an archaic word for drove meaning a horde, and is applied to swarming bees. The *Oxford Reference Dictionary* lists the word **bike**, which *Chambers Dictionary* defines as "a nest of wasps, wild bees etc.". It gives the alternative spelling **byke**, but apart from the suggestion that it is a Scottish term, the origins of it are unknown. The collective noun **grist** seems to be a fairly recent term applied to bees, appearing first in print around 1930. In addition to the word's definition as corn for grinding, it is an old American term meaning a portion or quantity, so would appear to have some validity as a collective noun. By far the most obscure collective noun for bees, however, is the term **erst**. This seems only to appear in the AA *Book of the British Countryside* and may be simply a modern example of miscopying (grist?) more evident in earlier mediaeval hand written manuscripts.

Although when one mentions bees many people think of the honey bee and the complex social structure of the hive, only very few of the thousands of different bee species are in fact social. Most of them are indeed known as "solitary insects" and have much the same sort of life history as other insect species.

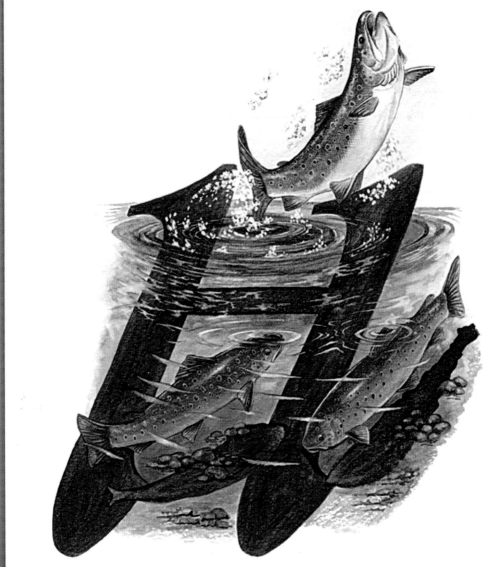

over
of trout

Anyone who has stood on the bank of a river or leaned over a bridge and, having accustomed their eyes to the play of light on the stones of the riverbed, identified the gentle tail-waving which betrays the position of a waiting trout, will identify with this most evocative of collective nouns. The definition in C E Hare's *The Language of Sport*, however, is rather less languid an image - it describes the term **hover** as an assembly of trout "waiting on the edge of fast water in great numbers ready to dash at food brought down by the stream."

A sea trout is sometimes called a *grey fish*, *whitefish*, *whitling*, *square tail*, *sewin*, *black neb* or *black tail*; trout newly emerged from the ova are called *alevin*; young fish of the whole salmon family are called *parr* after their umbilical sac is gone, but young sea-trout are also called *peal* or *herling*. A *finnock* is a young sea-trout which has not yet reached spawning age; a *smolt* is a young salmon or sea trout going to sea for the first time; a sea trout smolt is also called a *sprod* or *yellow fin*; a *grilse* is a fish on its first return from salt-water, sometimes called a *fork-tail*. A *pugg* is a third year fish. A *springer* is a fish returning to the river from the sea in spring and a *kelt*, *kipper* or *slat* is an "unclean" fish which has not recovered from spawning. A *baggot*, *shedder* or *rawner* is an unspawned fish after the usual spawning time, and a *maiden* is a fish which has never spawned. A large trout is sometimes referred to as an *alderman* and a *banker* is a trout lying up close to a bank. Got all that?

Kindle
of kittens

Cats (in the general sense) have six collective nouns which may be applied to them. In addition there are further collectives which apply to specific types of cats eg a *pride*, *sault*, *sowse*, *troop* or even *flock* of lions, or a *leap* of leopards. The six collective nouns relating to other cats are the "true term" *clowder*, the terms *destruction* and *dout* (sometimes wrongly copied as "dour") which apply just to wild cats, a *cluster* of domestic cats (sometimes appearing as *clutter*), a *glaring* of cats, obviously relating to the cats' eyes at night, and finally a *kindle* (sometimes written as *kinder*), a term which applies to young cats or kittens. All of these nouns have very early references in mediaeval literature, the most *recent* being the reference for *kindle* in *The Book of St Albans* of 1486. This term is also applied to young rabbits and hares.

Cats were probably first domesticated in the Middle East before the year 3,000 BC and there are now some fifty million of them in western European homes alone. They have been worshipped as gods, regarded as good-luck charms, as agents of witches and the devil, as well as being loved as household companions.

The British wildcat, looking rather like a largish tabby but with a much bushier tale, was once to be found all over Scotland, England and Wales. However, by the beginning of this century it seemed to be close to extinction, being confined to just a small area of Scotland. However, the wildcat managed not only to hold its own, but to increase its post-war range to the point where it is now regarded as relatively common in parts of Scotland. The wildcat's Latin name *felis sylvestris*, meaning cat of the woods, makes it the original "Sylvester".

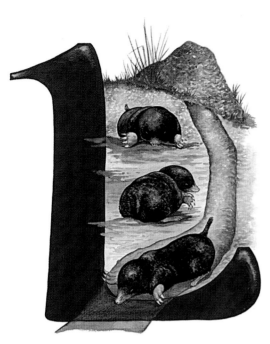

Labour of moles

Another evocative collective noun, a ***labour*** of moles conjures up images of the hard-working miners toiling underground for the common good. Moles seem always to have been regarded as industrious. In the seventeenth century John Dryden wrote :

> *The field-mouse builds her garner underground*
> *For gather'd grain the blind laborious mole*
> *In winding mazes works her hidden hole.*

The moles' industry is often evident above ground where the characteristic molehills indicate the activity below. Not always a welcome sight to farmers, the mole has long been regarded as vermin. In days gone by specialist molecatchers were a common feature of rural life. Not only did they kill moles for the farmer, the fur was in demand for two reasons - clothing and plumbing! The velvety, short, stiff fur of the mole is unusual in that it has no natural grain. It stands straight up, allowing the mole to move forwards or backwards in its confined burrow without ruffling its fur. It is also very dense to prevent fouling from soil or dirt. These qualities made the pelt of the mole attractive as a clothing material - particularly for moleskin breeches. Plumbers at one time also valued a moleskin to wipe smooth the tapered solder joint between two pieces of lead pipe. However, the molecatcher would also sometimes tie the trapped, dead bodies onto a gibbet, believing that this deterred any remaining moles.

An alternative collective noun for moles is ***company***.

Mute of hounds

Hounds, in keeping with other birds and animals associated with hunting, have a number of different collective nouns. A *leash* is a set of three hounds, especially greyhounds; a *couple* is a term for a brace of hunting dogs usually applied when they are running, while the word *brace* is itself another legitimate collective noun. Some authorities maintain that terminology for hounds generally should be differentiated from greyhounds specifically : two greyhounds a *brace*, two hounds a *couple*: three greyhounds a *leash*, three hounds a *couple and a half*.

The more general terms for an unspecified number of hounds include *pack* and *mute* (from Old French meute meaning pack or kennel, rather than any reference to a lack of vocalisation). The word *kennel* itself is a genuine noun of assembly for hounds as well as a place in which dogs live. *Kennel* is also the correct collective noun for dogs other than hounds. A *hunt* is both a group of hounds and a group of huntsmen, as well of course as the chase itself. A limited number of sources quote further collective nouns for a group of hounds as *cry* or *stable*. The term *litter* is used for a group of whelps or puppies.

A hound is defined as a dog of a kind used in hunting. A *sute* is a further collective noun for these dogs, although it has been quoted in some sources as a term just for bloodhounds. It comes from the word suite meaning a train of followers or attenders. A rache is a further sub-division of hounds meaning a hound which hunts by scent. C E Hare suggests that, along with *pack*, the term *kennel* should be used specifically for raches.

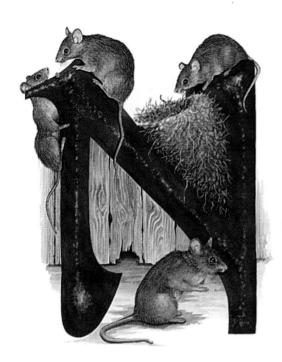 est
of mice

There are four species of mice in Britain. They are bright, inquisitive and successful creatures; the illustrated house mouse, for example, is found world-wide. It is not indigenous to Britain, though, and may have been the first mammal to have been introduced through human activity. Evidence shows that this mouse was certainly present in this country during the iron age, and it has always co-existed with humans. It steals our food, makes a home in our houses and keeps one genetic step ahead by developing immunities to many rodent poisons intended to bring about its downfall.

The most widespread and abundant mouse in Britain, however, is the woodmouse. Also known as the long-tailed field mouse, it is not as dependent on woodland as its name implies, being adaptable to many habitats. Indeed, it will readily follow the example of the house mouse and come into our homes during times of hard weather.

The yellow-necked mouse looks like a large woodmouse, which it was once considered to be. It is now regarded as a distinct species.

The harvest mouse is the smallest British mouse and perhaps the most appealing of the whole family. They live in meadows and hedgerows. The development of modern farming practices meant that the harvest mouse was in danger of becoming a great rarity, but it has clung on and is now even re-colonising lost ground.

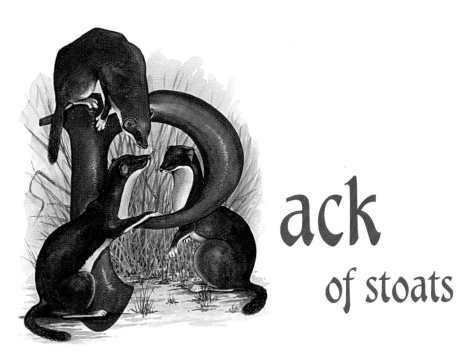

Pack
of stoats

Kenneth Graham's *Wind In The Willows* reinforced the image of stoats and weasels as the villains of the countryside: *".. a company of skirmishing stoats who stuck at nothing occupied the conservatory"*. Stoats, weasels and ferrets had occupied Toad Hall and the public, it seems, has never forgiven them.

The collective noun itself conjures up images of bullying gangs, but the often reported marauding **packs** of stoats are much more likely to simply have been family groups - there can be up to twelve young in a litter. Their lithe, almost snake-like bodies enable them to follow their prey down holes and burrows, and their sharp teeth and dark eyes complete the picture.

The folklore telling of them sucking blood in vampire fashion springs from their occasional killing method. Usually they kill with a bite to the back of the neck, but sometimes they will bite the throat of a rabbit and its death is not always instantaneous. Letting go would allow the rabbit to kick out, so injuring the stoat. It holds on, often getting blood on its face and coat in the process. The impressionable observer insists they have seen the stoat sucking the blood of another wild creature!

The stoat's black tail-tip distinguishes it from the similar weasel. To tell the two apart, it is no use relying on the old joke - "stoats are stoatally different while weasels are weasily distinguished"! The term **pack** is also applied to weasels, wolves, dogs and a predator of freshwater - the perch.

Pod
of whales

Pod is one of five collective nouns listed for whales. It is usually the one applied to smaller numbers of whales such as those making up a family group. The term is also referenced for hippotamus, seals and whiting particularly, but *Chambers Dictionary*, following its definition of *pod* as a *school*, goes on to say it is sometimes used for other groups of animals, fish and birds. Interestingly, the term *herd* is listed for sperm whales only and the *Oxford Reference Dictionary* includes the word *grind* as a noun of assembly exclusively for bottle-nosed whales. In addition to *school*, the other collective noun for whales is *gam* (see Gam of Porpoises).

Whales in recent times have captured the spirit of the modern conservation movement. Part of the reason for the public condemnation of whale hunting was not only the wish to protect the whale for its own sake, but also the growing realisation that the whale's intelligence was of a high enough order to render the killing methods unacceptable. Whales, like so many of the world's creatures, are not completely safe yet and there are still those nations which wish to hunt them, but they have gained significant protection - enough to allow for some optimism about their future. Great therapeutic benefit is claimed from time spent watching these gentle giants of the deep.

The illustrated killer whales, one of the toothed whale species and usually classified as dolphins, are fairly common and regularly seen in the seas around the northern British coast. The minke whale is the only baleen whale commonly seen in British waters. The commonest whale species to be found around Britain is the long-finned pilot whale, whilst the northern bottlenose whale and the sperm whale are rare sightings in deep waters.

Quantity
of smelts

This rather mundane collective noun is one of a fair number which are applied just to fish. Its reported origin is just as ordinary as the word itself: Isaac Walton, in his classic *The Compleat Angler* of 1676 refers to "vast **quantities**" of smelts coming up the River Thames in such numbers that even women and children began angling for them! The term subsequently stuck and appeared in later lists.

The origin of the smelt's name is rather more colourful. It is said that the name derives from the opinion of some that the body of the smelt bears the scent of violets. Whilst others have declared that the smell of the fish is that of cucumbers (an opinion supported by contemporary field guides), the principle of the smelt's natural aroma having influenced its name remains the same!

Although not members of the salmon family, smelts are salmon-like in a number of respects. They have, like salmon and trout, an adipose fin - a small fatty fin lacking rays which is situated between the tail and dorsal fin. Also like salmon and sea trout, smelts are anadromous, that is they return to spawn in freshwater rivers having spent their growing years in the sea. They do this in Spring, returning to the sea again after a few weeks or months to repeat the process again the following year. Sexually mature usually at the age of two to three years, they may spawn each year until they are fifteen years old.

RICHESSE OF MARTENS

RICHESSE OF MARTENS

 **ichesse**

of martens

The illustrated pine marten is the only marten native to Britain. It is a member of the large mustelid family which includes the otter, badger, weasel and polecat. Mustelids get their name from their habit of expelling supposedly musty-smelling secretions from scent glands under the tail. However, the scent of a pine marten is not unpleasant and its Old English name of "sweetmart" distinguishes it from its more evil-smelling relative - the "foulmart" or polecat.

The pine marten has a luxuriantly dense, rich chocolate brown coat with a characteristic creamy yellow throat bib. Consequently its fur was prized by royalty and nobles as a trimming for robes of state. Where once the pine marten was widespread across the tree-covered English landscape, it is now confined to a small area of Wales, Scotland and parts of Ireland.

Whilst generally shy, retiring and active mainly at night or at dawn and dusk, shunning human presence, they are known to come regularly to food in certain gardens (they have a special liking for strawberry-jam sandwiches!) and can be induced to take food even from the hand. I have seen a family group in a back yard during broad daylight, feeding on sandwiches right next to a window quite unconcernedly observing the watcher record them on video!

The collective noun is still sometimes written *richesse* in the same way as it appeared in print in mediaeval literature. The modern equivalent is *richness*. The term derives from the pine marten's rich fur. It has been incorrectly applied to the bird "martin" rather than to the animal "marten".

Smuck
of jellyfish

Appearing in different lists as **smuck**, **smack** or **stuck**, it seems likely that the collective nouns for jellyfish are all derived from the original printed version **smuck** contained in *Nuttall's Dictionary* of the 1920's. *Nuttall's Dictionary* itself defined the term as "a **crowd** of jellyfish", but whereas **smuck** and its derivatives found themselves in a number of subsequent lists - **crowd** did not appear again.

There is no record of how the terms originated. A smack is a small-decked fishing vessel in which there is a well for keeping live fish. It is unlikely, however, that jellyfish would have been kept in one. I like to think that the term's origin may rather have been onomatopoeic: something to do with the noise made when one inadvertently steps upon a stranded jellyfish on the beach, or perhaps the sound made when one might prod and lift it with a stick and part-suck its body like a plastic bag full of water from the wet sand - smmmuck! like a noisy kiss.

Whatever its origins, it is appropriate for there to be a collective noun for jellyfish: they are often to be seen drifting with the water currents in large groups. Indeed, many can often be seen stranded on the beach together, where they dry out and die.

The Common Jellyfish generally feeds on plankton, but larger jellyfish such as the illustrated Lion's Mane Jellyfish and the Compass Jellyfish feed on small fish and other animals which they trap with their stinging tentacles. Paradoxically, certain fish such as the whiting, which seem to be immune to the stings, take shelter and refuge amongst the tentacles.

Swarm
of eels

At first sight an unlikely collective noun for eels, the term *swarm* was first recorded in a book entitled *Rural Sports*, written in 1801 by Reverend W B Daniel. This became a standard work for hunting, fishing and shooting terms and therefore has some integrity. The term has subsequently been included in many lists. One of the dictionary definitions for *swarm* is a throng of small animals, particularly on the move. On reflection, therefore, it is a particularly appropriate noun of assembly for the young elvers which travel in their multitudes back to their freshwater homes.

The life history of the eel is now well researched and is one of those amazing stories which would seem to reside more in the world of fiction than fact. Eels spend up to nineteen years growing from immature yearlings in freshwaters of all types across Europe. They are known as "yellow eels" because of their brownish yellow colour. Ultimately changing colour to black and silver, the adults, known as "silver eels", make the journey of up to 7,000 kilometres back to the Sargasso Sea where they were born. The adults die after spawning in the spring, leaving the small, transparent "glass eels" to make their way back with the help of the Gulf Stream and the North Atlantic Drift to the freshwater homes of their parents. This journey is now thought to take about one year, when the whole amazing process begins again.

An old country superstition was that to put a live eel in a heavy drinker's glass of beer would cure him of his vice. It would certainly have put him off that particular drink!

TRIP OF HARES

TRIP OF HARES

Trip of hares

A traditional quarry species , the hare has nine associated collective nouns. This large number is in keeping with other birds and animals which are either used in hunting or else are themselves the hunted. Two of the nine are regarded as "true company terms". The first is *trip*, a term also applied to goats, sheep, pigs and dotterel. The second is *drove*, and may have been applied to hares because of the way in which they were driven during the hunt.

The term *husk* is apparently an old name for a company of hares, whilst a *trace* of hares refers to its footprint in snow. Regarding the origin of a *down* of hares, it is thought that different spellings such as *downe*, *dunne*, and *dun* may point to a comparison with the word "donie", an old country name for the hare. In his book *Language of Sport*, C E Hare (who I understand has no family connection to this animal), writes that the term *herd* is a miscopying from a "herd of hartes". In common with other animals of the hunt, the hare shares the collective nouns *brace* when referring to groups of two, and *leash* for groups of three individuals. The term *kindle* refers just to young hares in the nest.

There are two types of hare in Britain: the Common or European Hare (illustrated) and the Mountain Hare. Much folklore surrounds the hare. For example it was believed if one was seen by a pregnant woman, she would give birth to a baby with a hare-lip. Witches were once believed to turn into hares which then stole cows' milk, and could only be shot with a silver bullet.

WARREN OF RABBITS

Warren
of rabbits

This particular collective noun appears in just one list known to the author and yet its use as a company term is endorsed by the definition in *Chambers Dictionary*. This is in contrast to other more generally accepted collective nouns which appear in many lists but often have no contemporary dictionary references. Certainly the word *warren* is more commonly known as a series of interconnected rabbit burrows. *Colony* is also listed as a collective noun for rabbits, with the terms *kindle* and *nest* being applied to their young.

The term "rabbit" itself only referred to young animals until the eighteenth century, an adult being called a cony (or coney). Nevertheless it still seems surprising that lists of collective nouns often contain separate references for both. This is a tradition going back to the very earliest mediaeval manuscripts, where for example the Egerton manuscript lists the company term for conies as *bery*, now written *bury*, along with a listing for *neste* of rabbits. C E Hare suggests that as a corruption of "burrow" the term *bury* is properly the name of the conies' home and should not be regarded as a legitimate collective noun. Such an argument does not sit easily, however, with the definitions of *warren* above. Two conies are a *couple*; three a *couple and a half*. Many conies together have been termed a *fayre game* or simply a *game* of conies.

Rabbits share many of the country superstitions related to hares. To carry a rabbit's foot is thought to bring good luck. Good luck can also be achieved by saying "rabbits" three times on the first day of the month, although the charm loses its potency if it is not the first thing uttered early in the morning!

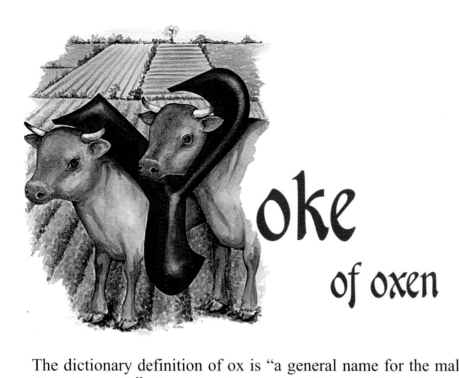

Yoke
of oxen

The dictionary definition of ox is "a general name for the male or female of common domestic cattle". The term, however, applies particularly to a castrated male, but has been extended to cover other animals of bovine type. The word oxen is, of course, simply the plural. Although an archaic usage of the term "cattle" related to horses and sheep, cattle in more recent times has clearly meant cows and bulls, or oxen. And yet, interestingly, lists of collective nouns nearly always differentiate between cattle and oxen. Some have even differentiated between cattle and "kine", simply a plural word for cows.

The group terms listed for oxen are *yoke*, *team*, *drove* and *herd*. Whereas the term *yoke* clearly relates to just a pair of oxen joined together under a frame of wood (modern dictionaries clearly specify definitions for the group term as well as the common noun), the word *team* is a more flexible number of animals pulling a plough or wagon. It is also applied to horses. A *drove* is a "true company term" also listed as a collective noun used for asses, cattle, hares, sheep and "beasts". Similarly, *herd* is a true company term. It is one of the most widely applied and its *listed* use is shared by antelopes, asses, bucks, buffaloes, cattle, chamois, deer, elephants, giraffes, goats, hares, harts, horses, porpoises, seals, shorthorns, swine, sperm whales and wolves!

Company terms for cattle are listed as *drove*, *herd*, *drift* and the Australian term *mob*. These terms are shared by "kine" in those lists in which there is a separate entry.

It would be more usual now to see a line of tractors rather than a *yoke* of oxen!

A List of Terms

Animals	*Menagerie*	**Donkey**	*Drove*
Antelopes	*Cluster, Herd, Tribe*	**Eels**	*Swarm*
Ants	*Colony, Army*	**Eland**	*Herd*
Apes	*Shrewdness*	**Elephants**	*Herd*
Asses	*Pace, Herd, Drove*	**Elk**	*Gang*
Baboons	*Flange*	**Ferrets**	*Business*
Badgers or "Greys"	*Cete, Colony*	**Fish**	*Shoal, Draught,*
Bears	*Sloth, Sleuth*		*Haul, Run, Catch,*
Beasts	*Drove, Flock*		*School, Aquarium,*
Beaver	*Colony*		*Cran, Flock, Leash*
Bees	*Cluster, Colony,*	**Flies**	*Swarm, Business,*
	Erst, Grist, Swarm,		*Cloud, Grist*
	Hive, Drift, Bike	**Foxes**	*Earth, Skulk, Leash,*
Boars	*Singular, Sounder*		*Troop*
Bucks	*Herd, Brace, Leash*	**Frogs**	*Army, Colony*
Buffaloes	*Herd, Gang*	**Geldings**	*Brace*
Butterflies	*Flight*	**Giraffes**	*Herd, Corps*
Camels	*Flock*	**Gnats**	*Swarm, Cloud,*
Cats	*Clowder, Cluster,*		*Horde*
	Clutter, Glaring,	**Goats**	*Trip, Herd, Tribe,*
	Dout , Dour,		*Trib, Flock*
	Destruction, Kindle	**Gorillas**	*Whoop*
Caterpillars	*Army*	**Grasshoppers**	*Cloud*
Cattle	*Drove, Herd, Mob,*	**Hares**	*Drove, Husk, Down,*
	Drift		*Herd, Trace, Trip,*
Chamois	*Herd*		*Brace, Leash,*
Clams	*Bed*		*Kindle*
Cockles	*Bed*	**Hedgehogs**	*Array*
Colts	*Rag, Rake*	**Herrings**	*Shoal, Glean, Army*
Conies (see rabbits)	*Bury, Warren, Fayre*	**Harts**	*Herd*
	Game, Game	**Hippos**	*Pod, Herd*
Coyote	*Pack*	**Horses**	*Harrass, Stable,*
Cubs	*Litter*		*Herd, String, Team,*
Curs	*Cowardice*		*Stud*
Deer *(all species)*	*Herd, Mob, Leash*	**Hounds**	*Brace, Couple,*
Dogfish	*Troop*		*Mute, Pack, Cry,*
Dogs	*Kennel, Pack*		*Stable, Hunt, Meet*

Hounds (cont'd)		**Pups**	*Litter*
(Greyhounds)	*Brace, Leash*	**Rabbits**	*Warren, Nest,*
(Bloodhounds)	*Sute*		*Colony, Kindle*
(Raches)	*Kennel, Pack*	**Racehorses**	*Field, String*
Impala	*Couple*	**Racoons**	*Nursery*
Insects	*Swarm, Plague,*	**Rhinoceros**	*Crash*
	Flight	**Roebucks/Roes**	*Bevy*
Jackrabbit	*Husk*	**Salmon**	*Bind*
Jellyfishes	*Smuck, Smack,*	**Sardines**	*Family*
	Stuck	**Seals**	*Herd, Pod, Rookery*
Kangaroos	*Troop, mob*	**Sheep**	*Flock, Hurtle, Drift,*
Kine	*See cattle*		*Mob, Trip, Drove,*
Leopards	*Leap, Lepe*		*Down*
Lice	*Flock*	**Shorthorns**	*Herd*
Lions	*Sault, Sowse, Pride,*	**Smelts**	*Quantity*
	Troop, Flock	**Snakes**	*Bed, Den, Knot*
Locusts	*Swarm, Cloud,*	**Spaniels**	*Couple*
	Plague	**Spiders**	*Cluster, Clutter*
Mares	*Stud*	**Squirrels**	*Dray, Drey, Colony*
Martens	*Richness, Richesse*	**Stoats**	*Pack*
Mice	*Nest*	**Swine wild**	*Sounder, Drift, Trip,*
Moles	*Labour, Company*		*Doylt, Herd*
Monkeys	*Troup, Cartload,*	**Tigers**	*Ambush*
	Tribe	**Toads**	*Knot, Knob, Nest*
Moose	*Herd*	**Trotters** (pigs)	*Nest, Set*
Mules	*Barren, Rake, Pack,*	**Trout**	*Hover*
	Span	**Turtles**	*Bale, Dule*
Mussels	*Bed*	**Vipers**	*Nest*
Otters	*Family, Bevy*	**Wasps**	*Nest*
Oxen	*Team, Yoke, Drove,*	**Whales**	*Pod, Gam, School,*
	Herd		*Run*
Oysters	*Bed, Hive*	(Sperm whales)	*Herd*
Perch	*Pack*	(Bottle-nosed)	*Grind*
Pigs	*Litter, Drove, Flock,*	**Weasels**	*Pack*
	Trip	**Whelps**	*Litter*
Ponies	*String*	**Whiting**	*Pod*
Porpoises	*School, Pod, Gam,*	**Wolves**	*Route, Pack, Herd*
	Herd	**Zebra**	*Herd*

Bibliography

Hare, CE	*The Language of Sport*	Country life, 1939
Partridge, Eric	*Usage and Abusage*	1947 - New and Revised Edition, Hamish Hamilton, 1965
Wildsmith,Brian	*Animals*	Oxford University press, 1967
Lipton, James	*An Exaltation of Larks or the Venereal Game*	Angus and Robertson Ltd, 1970
MacIver, Angus	*The New First Aid in English*	Robert Gibson, circa 1970
AA	*Book of the British Countryside*	Drive Publications, 1973
	The Oxford Reference Dictionary	Clarendon Press, 1986
	Complete Crossword Companion	Chancellor Press, 1988
ed. Stibbs,Anne	*Crossword Lists and Solver*	Bloomsbury Publishing Ltd, 1990
	The Chambers Dictionary New Edition	Chambers Harrap Publishers Ltd, 1993
Rees, Nigel	*Dictionary of Phrase and Fable*	Cassell, 1994
Browne, Philippa-Alys	*A Gaggle of Geese*	Barefoot Books, 1995